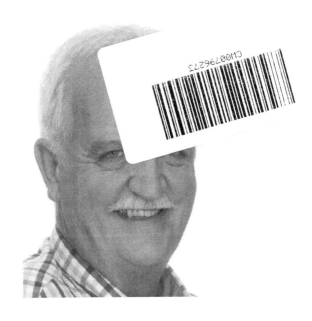

About me, the Author.

I'm David Reid, and I run my busy Hypnotherapy practice from my home in Odiham, Hampshire, and from The Farnham Natural Therapy Clinic in Farnham, Surrey. You'll find many more details about me on my websites www.DavidReidHypnotherapy.co.uk and www.MissionHypnotherapy.co.uk so I won't run through all that on this page.

I will say here though, that I'm a Senior Associate of the Royal Society of Medicine among my other qualifications.

At one time, I was also a Department of Transport Licensed Driving Instructor. For most of my life I've driven a great deal, and I reckon I've covered roughly 1,500,000 miles at the wheel. (Yes, one and a half million miles) I seriously doubt if there is another Hypnotherapist in the world who has done that. I still cover about 20,000 miles a year.

I've also driven various brands and types of vehicles, ranging from humble Minis to luxury Rolls-Royces, small and large vans, FWDs, SUVs, scooters, and even a 40-ton Peterbilt truck, and I've driven in England, Scotland,

Ireland, Wales, France, Belgium, Germany, Italy and New Zealand. I've driven in the rush hour in huge busy cities and in deserted country lanes, in beautiful sunshine, torrential tropical rain, in snow and ice, in 5-yard visibility fog, at all times of day and night, and in right and left hand drive vehicles.

These days, I'm a well known Hypnotherapist, specializing in Anxiety and Stress, Weight Loss, Stopping Smoking, Stopping Drinking and of course Road Rage and Anger Management, amongst many other things.

So I think you'll agree that I'm uniquely qualified to write a guide like this.

Take your time reading through it.

I'm sure you'll find it interesting – it might even save your life, or someone else's.

How to Reverse your Road rage – keep your cool and your licence.

"You will not be punished for your anger; you will be punished by your anger." ~Buddha

Introduction.

This is a short book. There's no padding in it. Road Rage is a serious condition and can cost you a lot in a lot of different ways. It can affect your health. It can get you beaten up. It can cause accidents, from minor all the way to fatal, for you or someone else. It can cause you to lose you licence, or to get penalty points on it. It can land you in jail with a criminal record. It can cost you financially through your insurance premiums, court fines or even losing your job. It can cost you your life. It can cost somebody else theirs.

Let me ask you this - -if you lost your driving licence tomorrow, and were offered the chance to buy it back the next day, how much would you be prepared to pay? £1000? £5000? £10000?

Buy this book instead.

CONTENTS

Chapter 1

Get ready to change gear

There's no point in reading this book and doing the exercises if you don't really want to change. Put it back on the shelf and save your money for those fines you'll soon have to pay. Having a positive attitude and taking a "can do" approach will get you further along the right road than anything else.

Since you haven't put the book back on the shelf, you're going to buy it, right? Attaboy! (or girl) That's step one already done. Now settle down somewhere quiet and read on.

You notice I said attaboy! first, not attagirl! Road rage is much more of a male phenomenon than a female one. There's no point in being all politically correct about it, it's just a fact. Men in general are naturally more aggressive and retaliatory than women, and aggression is a key feature of road rage. But the girls are catching up.

The point is, how are you going to change this bad habit you've got into? You think it's not a habit? You're wrong.

Any habit is an unconscious reaction to a situation encountered. Let's take cigarette smoking, one of the most common habits. The things that trigger the lighting up of a cigarette vary from person to person: here are some things that get people reaching for their cancer sticks.

Boredom

Tension

Stress

A perceived need to concentrate

Embarrassment

A gap in conversation

Peer pressure

Absent mindedness

This is far from an exhaustive list, I'm sure, whether you are or ever have been a smoker or not, you could think of many more.

I deal with helping people to successfully stop smoking very often. One of the key things is to help them realise what it is that triggers the habit at any given time, because most people have never given it much thought. Just getting them to be aware that they're reaching for a ciggy gives them the opportunity to choose NOT to reach for that ciggy before it's in their mouth and lit, by which time it's too late. You stop smoking one cigarette at a time.

How does this relate to Road Rage?

Since you now presumably recognise the condition in yourself – think about what triggers it in you.

Tension and stress might come to mind, but they're probably not the main causes. We all tend to be under quite a lot of tension and stress these days, but we don't all suffer from road rage. We'll cover the causes in the next chapter, but meantime, think about what triggers it most in you personally.

As a little incentive, think how often you've seen in the papers or heard on the news of a road rage incident where someone has been seriously hurt or even killed in a confrontation – beaten up, perhaps, stabbed or even shot. Here are some road rage statistics

• Britain is the top road rage country out of 16 European countries

• British drivers are the first to resort to making rude gestures to vent their anger.

• Britain had 80.4% of drivers claiming to have been involved in road rage. In

Holland 78.1%;

Greece 76.6%;

France 70% and

Germany 69.8%. [Gallup]

• 90% of drivers have experienced road rage.

• 60% admitted to losing their temper behind the wheel.

• 62% said aggressive tailgating was the most common form

• 59% said headlight flashing

• 48% said obscene gestures

• 21% said deliberate obstruction

• 16% said verbal abuse

• 1% said physical assault

[AA 1995]

• 1 in 4 adults has committed an act of road rage.

• Men are 3 times more likely to commit an aggressive act than women.

• 1 in 5 acts involved intimidatory driving, 61% verbal abuse, 50% aggressive hand gestures

• 30% of aggression is perpetuated by people in the 25-34 age group.

• 13 out of 1000 people were physically attacked and 24 had their vehicles attacked.

A follow up in 1998 found 84% believe the problem is getting worse.

• 50% of drivers have been victims of road rage [RAC 2000]

• 10mph is average traffic speed in London - 2 mph less than 1945. [Telegraph Oct '00), and it's been getting slower ever since.

• More than 1,000 people in the US die a year in road rage incidents.

US academic, James Strickland, found if provoked, motorists would respond by:

• 40% driving more aggressively

• 22% make angry expressions

• 15% mutter under breath

• 14% hit something in the car

• 5% obscene gestures

• 3% bump the car that was causing the anger

• Only 1 in 140 said they'd do nothing

If all that doesn't give you pause for thought, what on earth will?

Chapter 2

Now that you've paused for that thought, how did you get into this state?

It's not just on the road that we're all getting angrier. Air rage, PC rage, office rage, phone rage – they're all out there and coming your way if you don't do something about it.

You saw in the last chapter a lot of statistics about the causes, but what causes it in you?

Write down your top 5 gripes – your list might be something like this

- Someone causes you to almost have an accident, and then drives off laughing.

- An oncoming driver on a normal two-lane road barges out into the middle of the road past a parked car on his side, forcing you to swerve, brake or stop: by rights he should have given way.

- A heavy truck "uses his weight" to bully his way over into your lane on the motorway.

- Again on the motorway, someone comes up fast behind you flashing his lights and wanting to overtake.

- Someone nips in to a parking space ahead of you when you were obviously waiting for the chance to get in to it.

Your list might be a bit different.

The ones above all share a common theme though, and I bet yours do too – what is it?

THEY ALL FEEL LIKE A PERSONAL ATTACK ON YOU, THAT'S WHAT! This is what causes the upsurge of that feeling which can all too easily turn into ROAD RAGE.

Let's have a look at my five examples again.

• Someone causes you to almost have an accident, and then drives off laughing. Was this deliberate? – Unlikely. Do you know that person? – Again unlikely. Are you sure they were laughing at you, and not in relief that nothing actually happened? – Quite possible. Of course it COULD have been any of those things – but only could. After all, we all make mistakes occasionally, except you of course.

• An oncoming driver on a normal two-lane road barges out into the middle of the road past a parked car on his side, forcing you to swerve, brake or stop: by rights he should have given way. A tricky one to justify or excuse, this one. Of course it could be an expectant dad on his way to the hospital, but the chance are it's just lousy inconsiderate driving by some selfish boor, or more worryingly, someone completely oblivious to your presence.

• A heavy truck "uses his weight" to bully his way over into your lane on the motorway. Have you ever driven a heavy truck? It's not easy, and you have to time your manoeuvres well in advance because of your slow acceleration and large amount of space needed. Most HGV drivers are very good indeed. If this happens to you, the chances are that either you're so close to the front side of his vehicle that he can't see you in his mirrors, or so close to the rear of his vehicle before you pull out to overtake that he can't see you in his mirrors then either. The other thing that happens is that you come up on him so fast that he's already committed to his move before you become visible to him. The reality is, if you get into a collision with a heavy truck, you'll come off worst without a doubt, whoever's made the error. My advice is – don't get into any kind of dick-swinging contest. Give them the time and space they need.

• Again on the motorway, someone comes up fast behind you flashing his lights and wanting to overtake. If this sort of thing happens to you quite often – why? Are you in the habit of dawdling in the middle or outside lane for no reason? Are you creeping along at a needlessly low speed? Have you allowed yourself to be distracted by the radio, a passenger or a phone call (*see below) and slowed down unwittingly? Is the car behind an unmarked police car? The middle and outside lanes are both for overtaking, and you should drive in the inside lane unless you're doing that wherever possible.

• Someone nips in to a parking space ahead of you when you were obviously waiting for the chance to get in to it. Did the person who did this even see you waiting, even though your position was obvious? Were they driving a vehicle – for instance a van – with poor visibility?

(*Note on mobile phone use in the U.K. – other countries vary

Is hands–free phone equipment allowed? Yes, at the time of writing, provided that it can be operated without holding it. Pushing buttons on a phone while it is in a cradle or on the steering wheel or handlebars of a motorbike for example is not prohibited, provided you do not hold the phone. But again, should an accident occur, you can still be subject to prosecution.)

Chapter 3

Let go of old prejudices, or they'll still affect you

The so-called "reasons" for disputes leading to what we call Road Rage are actually triggers. In most human behaviour there is a stated and unstated, or conscious and unconscious, motivation for anything. The motivation for traffic disputes is no exception. While the event that sparks the incident may be trivial, in every case there exists some reservoir of anger, hostility, or frustration that is released by the triggering incident.

Old prejudices come into this a lot, and they're often nothing to do with driving.

How'd you feel about black people for instance, if you're not black yourself? If you are black, how d'you feel about patronizing whiteys treating you as if you're a gangsta? If you're a Muslim, how d'you feel about skinheads, say? If you're young, how tolerant are you of "doddery old gits" driving around slowly? And if you are one of the "doddery old gits", how do you feel about teenagers or others driving around with deafeningly loud music booming out of the open windows of their cars?

These are prejudices, whether conscious or unconscious, and we all have them, like it or not. (Even me, and no, I'm not going to tell you what they are!) Just because you're not aware of them doesn't mean they won't rise to the fore in certain situations.

However, if you are aware of them, that makes them much easier to control, so think about it. Be honest with yourself – you don't have to be politically correct here, you're only talking to yourself. (Incidentally, how d'you feel about mad people who go around talking to themselves?)

Once you've really and truly considered whether you have any of these inbuilt prejudices, you're on the way to better control of your reactions and emotions if you encounter people of that kind doing things that might annoy you.

Let's assume you're white, and not too keen on black people or loud music. You're driving along, and a black man pulls out in front of you suddenly causing out to brake hard and or swerve. He's also got his window wound down with reggae music blasting out. Pretty annoying, but something that happens quite often, especially in urban situations. So you're mildly annoyed now, and further down the road, he pulls in at the side of the road and stops. There's a space behind, and on the spur of the moment you pull in behind and jump out of your car to "have a word" with him. The very fact that you've done this shows that you're more annoyed than you probably should be right now. (Why?)

Unfortunately, it'll show in your body language as you approach your target. (Yes, your target – that's how your mind is working at this point). As you get right up to him and start to make your point, he's staring unblinkingly at you, which makes you feel he's being aggressive, and even worse, when he starts to reply, he doesn't look and speak directly at you but off to one side, and has a heavy Caribbean accent which you don't quite understand.

How d'you feel now? You're probably frustrated that you don't understand what he said, you don't like the fact that he isn't looking at you when he's talking to you, and you maybe feel he's being confrontational staring at you when you're talking to him. Of course you're not aware of any of these things consciously, but they all add to your annoyance to the point of making you angry.

Things can only go downhill from here.

Let's examine this situation a bit further. The other driver is black, and you're not keen on black people. Let me be clear here, I don't care about you're prejudices, likes and dislikes – I'm only talking about the effect they have on situations. He's also got reggae music blasting out of his car window and you don't like that either. By pulling out suddenly, he's directly affected your driving and driven off without acknowledging he's done anything wrong. These things are what started you feeling annoyed, aggrieved, irritated, call it what you will. If he hadn't pulled in just along the road, you'd probably have simmered for a while until either you or he turned off somewhere, and then gradually have forgotten all about it.

But if he hadn't been black with reggae music blaring out, what then? Say it had been a pretty young white girl with no music going? Would you have felt as annoyed – or even annoyed at all?

Another thing, Caribbean people often look away when they're talking to you, and tend not to blink much when they're looking at you: it's a cultural thing and they mean no offence by it, and because their skin is dark, their eye movement or lack of it is more obvious. OK, you still didn't understand what he said, but since you're a proud Geordie, did he understand what you said?

You see what I'm getting at here? OK, he misjudged things in the first place. On another day, you might never even have noticed, and were you travelling faster than the speed limit at the time anyway?

It's the fact that it felt personal (because it meant you're the one who had to take avoiding action), and therefore it was something that you didn't like done to you by someone who you had a predisposition not to like. Then compounded by the fact that he completely unwittingly appeared rude when you were trying to talk to him, and you felt embarrassed (yes, you felt embarrassed) that you didn't understand what he said.

No wonder problems can flare up suddenly from something so inconsequential!

But when you know the possible causes and acknowledge your own prejudices, things become much less fraught, and anger and confrontation much less likely.

Don't you agree?

Stereotypes come into it too when you're talking about prejudices – do you recognise any of these?

"The Hooded Horror" A 15-year-old Peugeot 206 or Renault Clio with only one hubcap. Paintwork dull red or blue, most side mouldings missing, dent in at least one door. There are usually at least 3 people in this car and it's usually seen late at night. You can't tell whether the driver or passengers are male (likely) or female (less likely), as all are wearing hoodies. Driven by Wayne, Del or Tel.

"The Rice Rocket" This is a Japanese or Korean car, usually the coupe version in white, black or red, has often had its suspension lowered and has a big bore exhaust about the diameter of a drainpipe hanging out the back. The body and bumpers are colour coded (flaking off), and the windows are black. The sides of the car are practically convex with the mind numbing thump of the stereo speakers inside, and once again you can't tell if the contents of this car are male (likely) or female (unlikely) because of the black glass. Also usually seen late at night. Also driven by Wayne, Del or Tel.

"The Girlie Car" Often quite new, and quite often a Fiesta, Clio, Corsa or similar. Vinyl flowers applied randomly on either the bodywork or glass, sometimes both. A festoon of small furry animals or jewellery (not furry) dangling inside from the rear view mirror stem. If you get close enough to this car, you might see the interior is knee-deep in old Coke cans, chewing gum and chocolate bar wrappers, plus hairbrushes and discarded gossip magazines. Very often just a lone occupant, lips moving as she chats on her Bluetooth to her mates as she wafts along. Seen at any time of day. Driven by Emily, Brittany or Courtney.

"The Cougar" A Lexus SC 430 convertible, or BMW 325 convertible, Maybe a Mercedes SL, in light metallic blue, white or silver. Immaculate, well-polished bodywork, and that's just the driver, who will be very visible apart from her eyes, which will be hidden behind large sunglasses to hide the crow's feet. Dripping in gold bangles and rings. Appears on sunny days only. The driver will be called Melissa, Pippa or Linda.

"Mr Smooth" Usually a Jaguar XK convertible or in more extreme cases an Aston Martin convertible. The driver will be good-looking, well groomed, tanned, salt and pepper haired, and reasonably slim. The car will not necessarily be spotlessly clean, and he will have a set of golf clubs in the boot. Don't you just hate him? Can be found in any prosperous country town, at any time of day, more prevalent near expensive hotels and golf courses. His name is Simon, Daniel or Jonathan.

"The Repmobile" More varied in car choice these days than it used to be, ranging from Astras and Focusses, through Mondeos and Vectras, to lesser BMWs, Mercs and Audis for the more senior staff. Usually driven quite quickly, decisively (some say aggressively), and purposefully. Will barge (from your point of view) out into queues of traffic, into the joining lane on the motorway, and will only get in to the single lane at the very last second when lanes are reduced for those never ending motorway roadworks. You might think the driver is arrogant – I couldn't possibly comment. But I know the driver's name, It's Ryan, Jeremy or Brandon.

There are many more examples that I'm sure you could come up with. Remember that just because you're a stereotype doesn't mean that people won't hate you on sight – what did I say earlier about prejudices?

Why not play the stereotype game down the pub with your mates tonight? See how many you can name.

Chapter 4

Moods and habits

When you set off to drive somewhere, what kind of mood are you in? A good one, or at least a neutral one, I hope. Starting to drive when you're already angry or feeling depressed or ill is a really bad idea.

All sorts of things can affect your mood before you even get in the car. Hunger, tiredness, elation, drink, drugs, your football team's performance, pre-menstrual tension, an argument with your partner, the weather, the temperature, jealousy, problems at work, problems at home, financial problems, your children fighting, your dog being sick, you feeling unwell, and many many more.

We all have stuff like this going on, and most of the time we cope pretty well with it all. But sometimes things get on top of us, and can really affect us for the worse – so beware.

This is another time when you need to stand back and take a long hard look at how you're feeling before you start off. It's not a sign of weakness – think of it as self-preservation if you like.

What can you do about it? Well let's have a think.

Obviously, try not to drive when your affected by any of the things mentioned a couple of paragraphs above, or any other factors that adversely affect your mood. Pretty impossible I hear you cry, and that's probably true. Modern life requires us to be pretty much mobile at the drop of a hat, and often that means driving. But if you're aware of the things which might be affecting you, you're in a much better position to prevent them from influencing you to act irrationally. Road rage is an irrational condition, after all.

Don't set off late, either; give yourself reasonable time to get where you need to be. That way, your mind will not be racing, and over sensitive to perceived problems along the way. Make sure you're not hungry, in particular, as if you are, your blood sugar will be low (not good for a variety of reasons) and your reactions will be that much poorer. Don't forget your glasses or contact lenses either, if you wear them – not seeing clearly doesn't help anything, and can contribute to misinterpretation of all sorts of things.

If you're a smoker, try not to smoke when you drive either. I used to smoke, and when the lit end of the cigarette fall between your legs when you're driving, it can have unexpected consequences. A sudden curl of smoke into your eye, or speck of hot ash, and suddenly you can't see clearly. In extreme cases, you might unwittingly set fire to a jacket on the back seat, like I did when I lived in New Zealand.

Select appropriate (don't you just hate that over used word?) music if you like listening as you drive, and play it at a sensible sound level. Def Leppard or Ozzie at 120 decibels is OK at home or in a club, but in city traffic? I suppose it could drown out the screams of the pedestrians you've just run over. Melodic, calm and soothing tunes help to tame the beast inside – classical music too, but not The Ride of the Valkyries or any bagpipe music.

Chapter 5

This is now!

It's pretty fashionable right now to practice "Mindfulness", and it's offered as a solution for anything from flat feet to cauliflower ears.

Do you know what Mindfulness is? – thought not. Basically it's living "in the moment" and it actually could help quite a lot with your Road Rage problem.

How?

Well, here are two definitions of mindfulness

A) "bringing one's complete attention to the present experience on a moment-to-moment basis"

B) "paying attention in a particular way: on purpose, in the present moment, and nonjudgmentally"

In a paper that described a consensus among clinical psychologists on an operational and testable definition, Bishop, Lau, et al. (2004)[9] proposed a two-component model of mindfulness: the first component involves the self-regulation of attention so that it is maintained on immediate experience, thereby allowing for increased recognition of mental events in the present moment. The second component involves adopting a particular orientation toward one's experiences in the present moment, an orientation that is characterized by curiosity, openness, and acceptance.[9]:232

Sounds a bit high-falutin', I know, but how can it help *you*? – and how?

Imagine one of the scenarios described earlier in Chapter 2. Someone causes you to almost have an accident, then drives off laughing.

Normally, lots of things flash into and through your mind when that happens, like "I could have been killed, there!", "What does that idiot think he's doing?", "What a tosser!", "Christ almighty, that was close!" "My heart's going like the clappers", "Bloody Hell" "Where're the pigs when you need them?", and many more, some of them involving castration or worse of the offender.

Using definition A above, your complete attention needs to be on the experience itself, not on the cause or the offender. You're still alive, your heart's beating faster, you're in control of your car, nobody's been killed or injured, and you now need to move because you're holding up the traffic behind. You can't actually do anything about what's just happened, all you can do is deal with right now, not what's past.

Using definition B, it's much the same, with the addition of not passing comment, even mentally, on other people's actions, i.e. the wanker that caused the problem in the first place. (Using mindfulness, of course, I wouldn't have been able to write that last bit, but I'm not currently trying to avoid page rage.)

Put more simply, just forget it, there's nothing you can do about it, what's past is past, and rehashing it in your mind won't change a thing. Here's the thing about incidents that have happened – there's no point in worrying about them because they're already history. Much better to concentrate on what's happening NOW, so you don't become part of history sooner than you expect.

We don't need to brand this common sense as "mindfulness" – it's just common sense, and you knew it already really. Sometimes though, you need reminded about it.

The chances are you'll never come across that person who almost caused the accident again anyway, but if you do, and if you're lucky, he might well be upside down in a ditch at the time.

Chapter 6

Change can be easy – try it

How often do you change your mind about something? Sometimes? Quite often? Seldom? All the time? Never? I bet you it's not the last one. We all change our minds all the time, and a good job too. Inflexibility is a sure sign of mental decay – look what happened to the dinosaurs. Well alright, giant meteorites hitting the Earth and changing the climate might have had something to do with it as well, but you get my point. And I don't see any giant meteors in tomorrow's weather forecast.

The world is fast moving, rules change, common practise changes, what's commonly acceptable alters all the time – not always for the better, it's true, but you certainly better be aware of it.

How up-to-date is your copy of the Highway Code? As I write, the latest edition was published in November 2012, with a revision in April 2014. It pays to keep yourself up-to-date with all the latest rules, regulations and recommendations. How do you know, for example, if something you've just done in your driving hasn't angered another driver who is more law abiding, or simply more knowledgeable than you are about current practice? Let he who is without sin cast the first stone, and all that.

A good example of recent perceived change is relevant to rule 264 (Motorway Driving) of the Code – the first two sentences of this rule are "You should always drive in the left-hand lane when the road ahead is clear. If you are overtaking a number of slower-moving vehicles, you should return to the left-hand lane as soon as you are safely past."

Recently, traffic police have started to enforce this rule much more frequently than in the past, and a good thing too. How often have you been stuck behind a middle or outside lane dawdler who has no reason to be there, since there's nothing in the inside lane to prevent him moving over? Even worse if it's in the outside lane that he's causing the obstruction. It's very, very tempting to move inside to overtake that way, isn't it? But pretty dangerous though – it's not referred to as "undertaking" for nothing.

I use the M25 quite a lot, and quite a bit of it these day is four lane. Even in the middle of the night, you find people driving along in lane 3, not even reaching 70 m.p.h., with no other traffic in site in any lane. Why are they doing this? It's worrying – are they asleep? What's even more annoying is that quite a few of them seem to be professional drivers, unless they've stolen the taxi or white van they're using.

 Of course you're not one of these people, I'm sure.

The point is that this sort of thing makes other drivers annoyed (a precursor of road rage), and is illegal. It's always been that way, of course, but if you're not up to date in your road knowledge, you might not be aware that it's going to be enforced more rigidly from now on – you can get done for it.

So **keep up to date with changes**, avoid fines and licence points, and don't annoy people and start making them angry. If everybody else did that, you wouldn't have any reason to get angry either, would you?

Chapter 7

Quick tricks in road rage situations.

You need to drop the anger fast, because that anger is doing you no good at all.

It certainly isn't changing the situation.

Instead of shrugging it off and getting on with your life, you're allowing that one discourteous act to take you from being happy and content to bitter and angry.

But what is a person to do? After all, the slight is perceived and the anger arises, unbidden.

I used to have that same struggle, but I found a cure and I can guarantee if you master this one simple technique, you'll banish road rage off to a corner of your mind where it will die a lonely death amongst the cobwebs.

So what's the trick, you ask?

As I implied, it's pretty simple (though not necessarily easy to master)

The next time another driver does something that stirs up the anger in you, do these eight things – they won't take long.

1. Take a really DEEP breath – breathing in for a count of 4

2. Hold the breath for a count of 3.

3. Release the breath slowly to a count of seven.

4. Do steps 1, 2 and 3 again.

5. Now, imagine a person you dearly love.

5. Imagine this person has just phoned and told you she/he is in desperate need of immediate assistance for an emergency situation and you are the only one who can give that help.

6. Imagine how you would be driving in that case.

8. Now, imagine the person who just provoked you with his/her bad driving is in exactly that predicament.

That's it!

Initially, your mind may start to rebel.

You may very well think it's more likely the person is just being an idiot. That might easily be the case, but can you actually know that?

(And isn't your angry response very "idiot-like" itself?)

Any number of situations could be happening in that person's life.

Is it a man whose wife is about to give birth and he wants to be with her? Perhaps it's a daughter whose father's just had a heart attack and she needs to get to the hospital to see him. Or maybe it's someone who's just lost her job and feels distraught. Of course it could be, it might be, just possibly, someone being a rude, ill-mannered slob.

The fact remains that a response of anger on your part only further upsets you and can even lead to acts of violence in extreme cases of road rage.

Nearly every time you get out on the road you will see another driver do something either discourteous or even downright dangerous.

Many times, you probably feel you are the recipient of that behaviour.

If you are anything like I used to be, your first impulse will be to blast the horn, swear, or put your pedal to the metal, try to pass the idiot and then cut him off.

Those of you who are less aggressive may at least find yourself hoping you'll come around the next bend and see that car off the road with a flat tyre—or, better still, see the bright blue flashing lights of a police car whose uniformed driver has pulled your new worst enemy over.

But is it worth it?

How much better is it to do what I just suggested and then, in a peaceful frame of mind, wish that person well and to get home safe – even if you have to swallow your pride to do that.

Wouldn't this world be a better place if we could all do this one, simple thing?

Chapter 8

Reinforcements are on the way – in fact they've arrived in this chapter, with 7 "Life Lessons" which should come in handy in any walk of life.

These are off-road techniques and advice to help you de-stress your life. Adopt or learn from some of this, and you'll be nowhere near as prone to road rage in the first place.

1   Keep your eyes on the prize.

This idiom means that you should keep your focus on achieving a positive end result. Anything you need or want to do can be thought of in more than one way. As an example, exercising can be described in "Prize" terms, like "getting healthier"—that's the reason, the "why" of exercising. Or try describing to yourself it in a more specific way, like "running two miles"—that's a method, the "how" of exercising. Thinking "Prize" about the work you do can be very vitalizing when you feel under stress and challenge, because you are linking one specific, maybe small and achievable action to a greater meaning or purpose. Something that may not seem particularly important or valuable – in fact potentially annoying - on its own gets cast in a whole new light. So when staying that extra hour at work at the end of an exhausting day is thought of as "helping my career" rather than "answering bloody emails for 60 more minutes," you'll be much more likely to want to stay put and do the job in a considerably more positive frame of mind.

2   Think like a Navaho Indian.

See your life in terms of progress – not perfection. The North American Navaho Indians are renowned rug weavers; tourist love to buy them. What's maybe less known is that the Indians always build in an imperfection to each rug. They do it so that they don't anger their Gods by daring to be perfect like the Gods are. It doesn't stop the Indians from selling loads of rugs. You needn't be perfect either, to succeed or live a happy life. Even Olympic athletes, who have to perform at their peak to win, can still make mistakes and win anyway. It's not necessary to be perfect either at work or at play so don't be so hard on yourself when things aren't absolutely flawless – the chances are you're the only one who even notices it anyway, and fretting about it is actually counterproductive. Just do your best, and accept that nobody ever – yes, you read correctly, nobody, ever – gets it right all the time.

3   Don't trip over molehills on the way up the mountain.

You might be extremely 'busy', but what exactly are you getting done in this frenzy of half-started and half-finished activities? Do you beat yourself up for being so bad at multi-tasking? If so, please stop. Research shows that trying to multi-task actually makes us less rather than more efficient.

If you continually try to micro manage every aspect of everything you do, you'll maybe get a lot of things right, but will you get the right result? The chances are you'll end up being side-tracked by things which are time consuming and which actually might divert your attention from the end product. In the workplace of course, depending on the industry you're in, superfine attention to detail might be vital, in which case that attention actually IS the end result for that detail at that time. For most of us though, it makes more sense to stand back a bit and ask the question "Will this action I'm considering doing really bring the end result nearer?" If it won't, why are you doing it? You don't need to continually juggle every aspect of whatever you're doing. Step back and really think about what's genuinely most important. You might even find that some of the things you were originally considering don't even need to be done at all! Don't forget to regularly refocus and reprioritize too – things seldom need to be cast in stone, and what was vital last week may be practically irrelevant this week. Having a clear sense of the order of importance of things very much reduces the stress of programmes and deadlines, and makes it a lot easier to avoid those molehills.

4   Look after your body

It's easy to forget to look after yourself when you're under pressure, even though you know you should. Time zips past so quickly when you have a lot to do that before you know it, another six months have disappeared without the reassuring knowledge that physically at least, you're OK. Preventive medicine is the aim here; early diagnosis and treatment of any possible problems right now can avoid potentially more serious situations in the future. Also, some physical conditions can adversely affect your performance without you realizing it. If you're already feeling under stress you can certainly do without something preventable causing that. The build-up of hormones released in the body by stress can cause lots of unpleasant physical symptoms such as a dry mouth, excessive sweating, rapid heartbeat, feeling "down", and disorders of the digestive system. Unfortunately, these symptoms can also be the start of various physical illnesses too, such as diabetes, stomach ulcers, thyroid malfunction and the like. Get yourself regularly checked out physically and don't assume things will go away by themselves – make sure. The certainty that all is well with your body will in itself reduce your stress levels.

5   Full English, please!

I don't want to sound preachy here, but what you shovel in to your body is so important. The current "great Satan" seems to be sugar, and it's certainly true that a great many modern processed foods contain far too much of it. However, they also often contain saturated fats, also pretty unhealthy in that they can contribute heavily to narrowing of the arteries, which in turn leads to circulatory problems, high blood pressure, strokes and heart attacks. Overloading your system with sugar, of course, can lead to diabetes, excess weight gain, depression, headaches and disturbed sleep, not to mention mood swings. Fast food is fine now and again, but it shouldn't dominate your diet. It's too easy to get into that fast food habit, just because it's, well, fast. Slow food is slower, but tends to be cooked from scratch because it's made from more elementary ingredients. They don't contain anything artificial, and your body will appreciate the fact that you know exactly what you're putting in it. The act of cooking can also be relaxing in itself. Too much caffeine from coffee and tea can make you feel jittery, hyper and anxious. Do I need to tell you about the effects of too much alcohol? – thought not. It might sound trite, it might seem self-evident, and you might have heard it all before, but the only real answer is a balanced diet and lack of excess. Don't turn into a health freak who only eats celery and figs though, that isn't a great idea either. Just be sensible and ask yourself these two questions - What's in what I'm about to swallow? What will it do to me once I've swallowed it? Studies have found that eating mackerel fish, for example, has a significant antidepressant effect, boosting energy levels and restoring feelings of calm and balance, and other feelgood foods include bananas, avocados, chicken, wholegrains and leafy green vegetables.

6   Give your backside a rest!

More preaching I hear you groan. No, just common sense really. Physical exercise releases endorphins into your body which is a natural way in which you can feel good. It only takes moderate exercise to make this happen, and when it does, you'll be amazed just how good you can feel in quite a short time. Endorphins originate mainly from your pituitary gland, although they affect and interact with receptors all over your body, and in fact there are more than twenty different kinds of them. Of course feeling good is an incentive to keep exercising, but don't overdo it, especially if you're not used to it. Another big benefit of exercising is the fat burning and weight control aspect. There's only one way to lose weight, and that's to use up more calories than you consume. Once you've lost that weight, keep it off by balancing what you eat with what you use, and you'll stay slim too. If you have a sedentary job, it's even more important. Just about all and any exercise helps, so use the stairs not the lift, walk to the station rather than drive or get the bus, take up cycling, swimming, tap dancing, krav maga or parkour if you're feeling exotic. You should always of course check with your GP before embarking on any new programme of exercise or weight loss, for your own peace of mind. Once you make a start on this, don't abandon it after just a few weeks, try to make it a regular feature of your life and specifically set aside some time for it each week. Make it a priority. Your stress levels will drop dramatically when you do. Not only that, you'll feel much more able to do your normal job and even feel good about it.

7   Who's more important than you?

Don't allow yourself to be at everybody's beck and call all the time. Quietly assert yourself in this respect. You wouldn't expect your colleagues, friends or family to drop everything to accommodate you (emergencies excepted of course), and they shouldn't expect it of you. Don't allow their priorities to dominate your priorities. You are entitled to respect as an individual, just as they are, and you have your own concerns to consider, whether professional or personal. If you let other peoples' problems become your problems, you'll NEVER be without problems – and how stressful is that? If you've allowed yourself to get into the unfortunate position where you've allowed this to happen, it can be quite difficult at the outset to change peoples' perceptions of you, but only at first. You don't need to be rude, or appear unco-operative, just be firm in expressing your take on what the situation is. Don't be afraid to be initially unpopular, if that's what it takes. You'll benefit from the satisfaction of having time to get on with what you need to do with fewer interruptions, so you'll get things done quicker and / or better. The satisfaction of that will in itself reduce your stress levels. You might find also that you're appreciated more by those around you as your confidence rises, which is pretty rewarding and stress reducing too.

Chapter 9

Driving to the future

If you've got this far, you're obviously pretty serious about doing something positive about your old tendency to road rage – that's great isn't it?

You've also read and (hopefully) absorbed a lot about the statistics, probable causes, effects and alternative ways to think about the phenomenon.

In spite of all that, you might still encounter the odd moment when the red mist rises – so what to do when it does?

If you feel rage building up in yourself

1. Firstly, don't do anything in haste – think before you act.

2. Breathe – see Chapter 7, steps 1 to 4

3. Use your imagination to change your perception of the situation – see Chapter 7, steps 5 to 8.

4. Stay in your seat, but consciously relax your grip on the wheel.

5. Say to yourself (out loud if you need to) "What's the point?"

6. Think of your anger as a coloured rubber ball (most people choose red for this), and see it in your mind's eye bouncing high, then lower, then lower again and so

on as your anger diminishes and gets further away as the ball rolls off into the distance. As it does so, fade the colour to grey in your mind.

If you are the subject of someone else's road rage

1. Stay in your seat, but consciously relax your grip on the wheel.

2. Consider – have I done something to provoke the other person's anger? (don't discount this – you might easily have done so without realizing)

3. Think about what you're going to do when you're out of this traffic situation – at home, with your wife/girlfriend/boyfriend/dog etc.

4. See the funny side. Imagine the angry person as a goldfish behind glass through the windows of their car, mouthing away silently. But don't actually laugh, that will likely just make things worse.

5. If the worst comes to the worst, and the person gets out of his car and marches towards you, still stay in your seat, make sure the doors are locked and the windows are up. Visualize the person being in a clown outfit with spotty bow tie, huge shoes, baggy trousers etc. You'll find it pretty hard to be angry back if you do this.

6. Even with point 4 and 5, remember that the other person is a human being just like you. Even if they are suffering from road rage, remember you don't have to. Your aim now is to defuse the situation and get out alive.

A couple of more general points now, before you set off, to reduce the likelihood of either becoming enraged yourself, or enraging others.

Plan ahead, both for the actual journey and for your reason for making it. You'll be more relaxed and more able to concentrate on your driving when you do,

Don't be competitive on the road. Your car is not actually an extension of yourself, no matter how much the advertiser's copy works to persuade you that it is. And it's most definitely not a weapon.

Remember what I said about music? Not too loud, no heavy metal – stick to easy listening, jazz, or classical. Who knows? – it might broaden your taste too, if that's not your usual diet.

Make sure your car is in good condition, and you have enough fuel and screenwash to get you there.

Ensure the seat is adjusted comfortably for you – don't try to change it on the move.

And that's it for this chapter

Chapter 10

Back on the road

Here's a quick checklist now before I go, and before you set off on your next trip.

Ask yourself if any of these statements apply to you? Be honest and answer yes or no.

I often exceed the speed limits so that I can get to work on time.

I drive up close to the driver in front, particularly if they are hogging the middle or outside lane.

I have a tendency to often flash my lights and blast my horn to let other drivers know they've annoyed me.

I verbally abuse other drivers even if I know they can't hear me.

I mutter and grumble under my breath about other drivers.

I often weave in and out of traffic to gain a small advantage.

I feel the need to put other drivers straight about what they have just done.

My passengers quite often tell me to calm down.

I drive better than most others on the road.

Those were comparatively mild – here are a few worse ones

I close up gaps in my lane, to stop other people getting in.

I jump traffic lights on yellow, because I get impatient waiting at red lights.

I sometimes make visibly insulting physical signs at drivers who annoy me.

I criticize other drivers out loud to my passengers.

I fantasize about physically assaulting other drivers.

I race past other drivers and cut sharply in front of them in retaliation.

I force other drivers to give way, when by rights I should have done.

And here are some really bad ones.

I frighten my passengers with my behaviour.

I throw things at other cars.

I carry a weapon in my car,

I'm quite willing to physically assault another driver.

I use my car as a weapon or to intimidate.

If you answered "Yes" to any of these, go back and read this book again, and pay more attention this time. When you get back to this chapter, run through all these questions again, but this time put the word "Will" before each one, and a question mark at the end. "Will" I feel the need to put other drivers straight about what they've just done?" "Will" I throw things at other cars?)

Have you done that? Better this time? – Good.

I hope what you've read and practised as a result of reading this little book has helped your understanding of your own and others' behaviour on the road. Please let me know if it's done that, and if you've enjoyed it.

You can contact me at David@DavidReidHypnotherapy.co.uk

I've only one more thing to say to you before I go

When you get back out on the road – BE CAREFUL OUT THERE.

Please visit my websites

www.DavidReidHypnotherapy.co.uk

and

www.MissionHypnotism.co.uk

· for much more information.

Hypnotherapy, NLP and Life Coaching can help you get the most out of life, simply my making small changes in the way you think.

I've helped loads of people, just like you, to do exactly that, and I can help you too.

There'll be no psycho-babble, no crystals and incense, and no magic or mysticism.

There will be an honest and pragmatic approach, with a clearly set out and expressed plan of treatment, with a targeted result in mind. It's enjoyable too.

Not all Hypnotherapists are alike, so choose carefully.